THE PARTY OF HELL NO

THE REPUBLICANS ARE TALKING, YOU SHOULD BE LISTENING

By

DIANNE DICKEL AND GLENN DICKEL

An American mom and son project
Los Angeles, CA
The Party of Hell No, 2010
www.thepartyofhellno.net

Dedicated To:

REPUBLICANS AND FOR WHICH THEY STAND

Dick Cheney

"THE Obama administration is dithering on a decision about whether to send more troops to Afghanistan."

» What is he: Previous Vice President
» Where is he from: Wyoming
» Date of quote: October 22, 2009

Source: The Caucus. The Politics and Government Blog of The Times

Glenn Beck

"I'M thinking about killing Michael Moore, and I'm wondering if I could kill him myself, or if I would need to hire somebody to do it. ... No, I think I could. I think he could be looking me in the eye, you know, and I could just be choking the life out. Is this wrong?"

» What is he: Host, The Glenn Beck Program
» Where is he from: Fox Cable News
» Date of quote: May 17, 2005

Source: Broadcast of the Glenn Beck Program

Joe Lieberman

"IF we did what Sen. Obama wanted us to do last year, Al-Qaeda and Iran would be in control of Iraq today. The whole Middle East would be in turmoil and American security and credibility would be jeopardized."

> » What is he: U.S. Senator
> » Where is he from: Connecticut
> » Date of quote: April 3, 2008

Source: Fox News - Picture above... Joe Lieberman campaigning for the GOP during the 2008 election with Sarah Palin... Photograph: Chris O'Meara/AP

Michael Steele

"MY intent was not to go after Rush – I have enormous respect for Rush Limbaugh." "I was maybe a little bit inarticulate. ... There was no attempt on my part to diminish his voice or his leadership."

» What is he: Republican National Committee Chairman
» Where is he from: Maryland
» Date of quote: March 2, 2009

Source: Saturday night: Steele told CNN host D.L. Hughley in an interview "Rush Limbaugh is an entertainer. Rush Limbaugh — his whole thing is entertainment. He has this incendiary — yes, it's ugly."

Rush Limbaugh

"OBAMA'S got a health care logo that's right out of Adolf Hitler's playbook ... Adolf Hitler, like Barack Obama, also ruled by dictate."

» What is he: Radio host
» Where is he from: Missouri
» Date of quote: August 6, 2009

Source: Rush Limbaugh Show

Michele Bachmann

"WE'RE in a state of crisis where our nation is literally ripping apart at the seams right now, and lawlessness is occurring from one ocean to the other. And we're seeing the fulfillment of the Book of Judges here in our own time, where every man doing that which is right in his own eyes—in other words, anarchy."

» What is she: U.S. Congresswoman
» Where is she from: Minnesota
» Date of quote: March 6, 2004

Source: guest on radio program "Prophetic Views Behind The News", hosted by Jan Markell, KKMS 980-AM

Lamar Alexander

"WITH respect, you (Obama) are wrong about your bill. It would increase premiums, I believe."

- » What is he: Senator
- » Where is he from: Tennessee
- » Date of quote: February 25, 2010

Source: WASHINGTON, (Reuters) at Healthcare Summit

Dr. Tom Coburn

"I favor the death penalty for abortionists and other people who take life."

» What is he: U.S. Senator
» Where is he from: Oklahoma
» Date of quote: December 14, 2004

Source: http://www.washingtonpost.com/wp-dyn/articles/A62348-2004Dec13.html

Jim DeMint

"HOMOSEXUALS and unmarried, pregnant women should not teach in public schools."

- » What is he: U.S. Senator
- » Where is he from: South Carolina
- » Date of quote: October 6, 2004

Source: On the issues ttp://www.massscorecard.org/Domestic/Inez_Tenenbaum_Civil_Rights.htm

Mike Pence

"I never thought I'd live to see the day that an American administration would denounce the Jewish State of Israel for rebuilding Jerusalem."

» What is he: U.S.Congressman
» Where is he from: Indiana
» Date of quote: March 23, 2010

Source: http://eyeonfreedom.com/index.php/%E2%80%9Ci-never-thought-i%E2%80%99d-live-to-see-the-day-that-an-american-administration-would-denounce-the-jewish-state-of-israel-for-rebuilding-jerusalem%E2%80%9D/

2nd Source: http://blogs.cbn.com/beltwaybuzz/archive/2010/03/23/stop-bullying-israel-and-focus-on-iran.aspx

John Cornyn

"THE caution we try to preach to everyone is that just because the public has fallen out of love with the president and his policies doesn't mean they've fallen in love with Republicans."

» What is he: U.S. Senator
» Where is he from: Texas
» Date of quote February 22, 2010

Source: *Reuters* Cornyn told POLITICO. tpmdc.talkingpointsmemo. com/2010/02/senate-to-hold-key-test-vote-on-scaled-down-jobs-bill.php

Rudy Giuliani

"HILLARY and Obama are kind of debating whether to invite them to the inauguration or the inaugural ball." –on Osama bin Laden and Mahmoud Ahmadinejad.

» What is he: 2008 Republican presidential candidate
» Where is he from: New York
» Date of quote: October 29, 2007

Source: http://www.huffingtonpost.com/2007/10/29/giuliani-unhinged-hillary_n_70353.html

Karl Rove

"I don't think she (Michelle Obama) did too well on saying I love America. That wasn't adequate enough."

» What is he: President George W. Bush's chief strategist
» Where is he from: Colorado
» Date of quote: August 26, 2008

Source: Interview, Fox News with host Brit Hume

Mitt Romney

"LINDSAY Vonn's downhill gold had been stripped because, "It was determined that President Obama is going downhill faster than she is."

» What is he: Former Governor
» Where is he from: Massachusetts
» Date of quote: February 18, 2010

Source: http://blogs.abcnews.com/thenote/2010/02/romney-introduced-by-surprise-scott-brown-at-cpac-sounds-like-a-presidential-candidate.html

Tim Pawlenty

"THEY should be focused like a laser on jobs, not acting like a manure spreader in a wind storm,."

- » What is he: Governor
- » Where is he from: Minnesota
- » Date of quote: November 8, 2009

Source: http://www.politico.com/news/stories/1109/29285.html

Carl Paladino

FACT....Paladino forwarded Email of President Obama Depicted as a Pimp and Michelle Obama dressed as a prostitute.

» What is he: GOP race for Governor
» Where is he from: New York
» Date of source: April 11, 2010

Source: The Buffalo News http://buffaloescortsnews.com/page/3

2nd Source:http://tpmmuckraker.talkingpointsmemo.com/2010/04/tea_party_gov_candidates_racist_sexually_graphic_e.php

Sarah Palin

"THE America I know and love is not one in which my parents or my baby with Down Syndrome will have to stand in front of Obama's 'death panel' so his bureaucrats can decide, based on a subjective judgment of their 'level of productivity in society,' whether they are worthy of health care. Such a system is downright evil."

» What is she: Former Governor
» Where is she from: Alaska
» Date of quote: August 7, 2009

Source: Sarah Palin's Facebook Page

2nd Source: http://www.huffingtonpost.com/2009/08/07/palin-obamas-death-panel_n_254399.html

Zell Miller

"THERE is but one man to whom I am willing to entrust their future and that man's name is George W. Bush."

» What is he: Former U.S Senator
» Where is he from: Georgia
» Date of quote: September 1, 2004

Source: http://www.cnn.com/2004/ALLPOLITICS/09/01/gop.miller.transcript/..Wednesday, September 1, 2004 Posted: 11:18 PM EDT (0318 GMT) NEW YORK (CNN)

Newt Gingrich

"THE left has a very temporary moment in history when it has both Congress and the White House, I think we will repeal virtually everything they did."

» What is he: Former Speaker of the U.S. House of Representatives
» Where is he from: Pennsylvania
» Date of quote: March 22, 2010

Source: Southern Republican Leadership Conference

Mitt Romney

"LIBERAL neo-monarchists."

» What is he: Former Governor
» Where is he from: Massachusetts
» Date of quote: February 18, 2010

Source: http://answers.yahoo.com/question/index?qid=2010022309
0411AAohVOm...*ABC News*

Bobby Jindal

"DEMOCRATS have taken a fundamentally dishonest approach to reform. Obama is "repeating the mistakes" of Hillarycare, forcing Americans to join a public plan, diminishing the quality of services, and raising middle-class taxes. They might as well try to argue that up is down,."

»   What is he: Governor
»   Where is he from: Louisiana
»   Date of quote: July 22, 2009

Source: Wall Street Journalhttp://www.newser.com/story/64984/jindal-slams-dishonest-health-plan.html

Mitch McConnell

"THE debt they ran up in the first year of the Obama administration is bigger than the last four years of the Bush combined."

» What is he: Senate Minority Leader U.S. Senator
» Where is he from: Kentucky
» Date of quote: February 4, 2010

Source: Live Interview on Fox News

Ben Stein

"MR. Obama could become president and derail everything because his understanding of economics is 100 percent wrong. ... I must say I'm so scared about Mr. Obama becoming president. I can hardly tell you."

» What is he: Actor, Writer and Lawyer
» Where is he from: Washington D.C.
» Date of quote: February 14, 2008

Source:http://blogsforvictory.com/2008/02/15/ben-stein-obama-will-be-real-dangerous/ Kudlow & Company.

Karen Hughes

"AND, you know, I tell young people today that I've never vested in a single retirement plan any place I've ever worked."

» What is she: Former Under Secretary of State
» Where is she from: Texas
» Date of quotes: 1994–2009

Source: http://www.quotes-museum.com/quote/42715

Jon Voight

"I'M here to validate all the millions of people who are opposed to the Obama health care, we're witnessing a slow and steady takeover of our true freedoms. We're becoming a socialist nation, and Obama is causing civil unrest in this country."

» What is he: Actor
» Where is he from: New York
» Date of quote: September 2, 2009

Source: http://www.examiner.com/x-14650-Entertainment-

Andre Bauer

"THE problem is we have a giveaway system in this country and in this state that is so strong that people would rather sit home and do nothing than do these jobs. Laziness is not a disability. There are a lot of people that are flat out lazy and they are using up the goods and services that we have in this state."

» What is he: Lt. Governor
» Where is he from: South Carolina
» Date of quote: April 23, 2010

Source: http://www.independentmail.com/news/2010/apr/23/
bauer-blames-illegal-immigration-lazy-south-caroli/

Mark Sanford

FACT...Formerly employed by Goldman Sachs.

» What is he: Governor
» Where is he from: South Carolina
» Date of his employment: 1983

Source: http://www.washingtonpost.com/wp-dyn/content/
article/2008/09/25/AR2008092503602.html

Della Montgomery & Stephanie Chretienis

FACT...Birthright Citizenship Alignment Act...A proposed ballot initiative to refuse United States' citizenship to children born from foreign parents residing in Arizona.

» What are they: Protesters against The Fourteenth Amendment to the United States Constitution
» Where are they from: Arizona
» Date of source: December 4, 2007

Source: http://immigrationbuzz.com/?p=1504

Birthright Citizenship Political Committee is chaired by Della A. Montgomery and Stephanie Chretien

Mike Huckabee

"WHEN we were in college we used to take a popcorn popper – because that was the only thing they would let us have in the dorms – and fry squirrels in the popcorn popper."

» What is he: Former Governor
» Where is he from: Arkansas
» Date of source: January 25, 2008

Source: http://politicalhumor.about.com/od/mikehuckabee/a/ huckabeequotes.htm

2nd Source: http://politicalhumor.about.com/od/mikehuckabee/ youtube/huckabeepop.htm

Russell Pearce

(right) Russell Pearce with close friend   JT Ready with his Nazi family.
neo-Nazi J.T. Ready.

FACT...Pearce introduced a bill that would require a copy of the *Ten Commandments* to be placed on the front entrance of the original 1898 state Capital building by Jan.1, 2011.

- » What is he: U.S Senator
- » Where is he from: Arizona
- » Date of source: January 27, 2010

Source:http://www.azcentral.com/news/election/azelections/articles/2010/01/27/20100127politics-brief0127.html

Photos and story, By Stephen Lemons http://blogs.phoenixnewtimes.com/bastard/2007/09/russell_pearces_willie_horton.php

Russell Pearce

FACT... Pearce is the author of the Arizona bill SB 1070/HB 2632. *SB 1070* would require police to make a "reasonable attempt" to determine the immigration status of anyone they come into contact with during an investigation. And it would make the mere presence of an illegal immigrant anywhere in Arizona a violation of state trespass laws. This is without any training or supervision by federal authorities.

» What is he: U.S Senator
» Where is he from: Arizona
» Date of source: February 16, 2010

Source: http://azdailysun.com/news/state-and-regional/ article_6d238b07-d3f4-57d2-ae17-c31c56897517.html

Photos and story, By Stephen Lemons http://blogs.phoenixnewtimes. com/bastard/2007/09/russell_pearces_willie_horton.php

Andy Williams

"OBAMA is following Marxist theory. He's taken over the banks and the car industry. He wants the country to fail."

»   What is he: Former Singer, and Republican contributor
»   Where is he from: Iowa
»   Date of quote: September 30, 2009

Source: http://scienceblogs.com/dispatches/2009/09/andy_williams_
bashes_obama_on.php http://www.contactmusic.com/pics/lb/music_
cares_070209/andy_williams_2277851.jpg

Karl Rove

"I think it was inappropriate, look, a slight nod of the head perhaps to the Japanese Emperor, what's that all about, I mean he's not even the Head of State, but that deep bow from the waist actually from the Japanese culture speaks weakness, and look the President of the United States (Obama) simply can't get it right."

» What is he: Former President George W. Bush's chief strategist
» Where is he from: Colorado
» Date of quote: November 16, 2009

Source: http://www.youtube.com/watch?v=_UdP64CgsDk&feature=player_embedded

Charles Krauthammer

"OBAMA last night sounded smooth, polished, strong and convincing, and what he was selling was snake oil."

» What is he: Columnist and political Commentator
» Where is he from: The Washington Post
» Date of quote: September 11, 2009

Source:http://www.realclearpolitics.com/video/2009/09/11/
krauthammer_slams_speech_obama_is_selling_snake_oil.html

Michele Bachmann

(At a rally against same-sex marriage) "IT will be an awesome day. We are going to be beseeching the Lord."

» What is she: U.S. Congresswoman
» Where is she from: Minnesota
» Date of quote: March 20, 2004

Source: http://www.thebachmannrecord.com/thebachmannrecod. html// Prophetic Views Behind The News", hosted by Jan Markell, KKMS 980-AM, March 20, 2004.

Andre Bauer

"MY grandmother was not a highly educated woman, but she told me as a small child to quit feeding stray animals. You know why? Because they breed! You're facilitating the problem if you give an animal or a person ample food supply. They will reproduce, especially ones that don't think too much further than that."

» What is he: Lt. Governor
» Where is he from: South Carolina
» Date of quote: January 23, 2010

Source: http://www.independentmail.com/news/2010/apr/23/bauer-blames-illegal-immigration-lazy-south-caroli/

2nd Source: http://www.cbsnews.com/8301-503544_162-6139186-503544.html

John McCain

"THE Americans have gotten to know Sarah Palin. They know she's a role model to women and reformers all over America."

» What is he: U.S. Senator
» Where is he from: Arizona
» Date of quote: October 16, 2008

Source: http://www.telegraph.co.uk/news/newstopics/ uselection2008/presidentialdebates/3207208/US-presidential-debate-John-McCain-and-Barack-Obama-in-quotes.html....Telegraph. co.uk

Sarah Palin

"THEY are kooks, so I agree with Rush Limbaugh. Rush Limbaugh was using satire ... I didn't hear Rush Limbaugh calling a group of people whom he did not agree with 'f-ing retards,' and we did know that Rahm Emanuel, as has been reported, did say that. There is a big difference there."

» What is she: Former Governor
» Where is she from: Alaska
» Date of quote: February 7, 2010

Source: FOX News Sunday interview (Sarah Palin attempting to rationalize why it's okay for Limbaugh to use the word "retards" but not Emanuel)

Lynn A. Westmoreland

"JUST from what little I've seen of her (Michelle) and Mister Obama, Senator Obama, they're a member of an elitist class individual that thinks that they're uppity."

» What is he: U.S. Congressman
» Where is he from: Georgia
» Date of quote: September 14, 2008

Source: Lynn Westmoreland, left, during a 2003 vote on the Georgia flag at the Capitol in Atlanta. (AP/Gregory Smith)

John McCain

"DO you know why Chelsea Clinton is so ugly? Because Janet Reno is her father."

» What is he: U.S. Senator
» Where is he from: Arizona
» Date of quote: June 1998

Source: http://state29.blogspot.com/2007/02/do-you-know-why-chelsea-clinton-is-so.html.... Republican Senate fundraiser in 1998.

2nd Source: http://anti-state.com/forum/index.php?board=1;action=display;threadid=20490

3rd Source: http://answers.yahoo.com/question/index?qid=20080905220253AARcMIi

Dan Burton

"WITH the American people increasingly behind us, the Republican Party will forcefully continue the fight against the President's socialist policies."

» What is he: U.S Congressman
» Where is he from: Indiana
» Date of quote: January 15, 2010

Source:http://www.facebook.com/notes/danny-burton/burton-responds-to-obamas-war-cry/297526127456

Steve King

"YOU are the awesome American people, If I could start a country with a bunch of people, they'd be the folks who were standing with us the last few days. Let's hope we don't have to do that! Let's beat that other side to a pulp! Let's chase them down. There's going to be a reckoning!"

- » What is he: U.S. Congressman
- » Where is he from: Iowa
- » Date of quote: March 22, 2010

Source : Tea Partiers on Capitol Hill...http://thinkprogress. org/2010/03/22/king-health-secession/

Mark Sanford

"I think it would be much better for the country and for him [Livingston] personally (to resign). I come from the business side. *If you had a chairman or president in the business world facing these allegations, he'd be gone.*"

» What is he: Governor
» Where is he from: South Carolina
» Date of quote: June 25, 2009

Source: Reuters http://www.leadershipturn.com/quotable-quotes-the-hypocrisy-of-mark-sanford/

2nd Source:http://www.leadershipturn.com/quotable-quotes-the-hypocrisy-of-mark-sanford/

Rudy Giuliani

"OBAMA'S vision "inept," a liberal fantasia."

»   What is he: 2008 Republican presidential candidate
»   Where is he from: New York
»   Date of quote: April 6, 2010

Source: interview with The National Review

2nd Source: http://dailyradar.com/beltwayblips/story/giuliani-an-inept-president-s-left-wing-dream/

Newt Gingrich

"I hope that the girls love the dog. I hope the family and all the pressure they're going to be in finds it useful. And I think that this whole thing is fairly stupid."

» What is he: Former Speaker of the U.S. House of Representatives
» Where is he from: Pennsylvania
» Date of quote: April 12, 2009

Source: http://politicalticker.blogs.cnn.com ABC's "This Week."

John McCain

"I spent several years in a North Vietnamese prison camp, in the dark, fed with scraps. Do you think I want to do that all over again as vice president of the United States?"

» What is he: U.S. Senator
» Where is he from: Arizona
» Date of quote: May 29, 2004

Source: late-night TV show on Conan O'Brien

Sarah Palin

"ALL of 'em, any of 'em that have been in front of me over all these years." (When asked to name a single newspaper or magazine she reads)

» What is she: Former Governor
» Where is she from: Alaska
» Date of quote Oct 1, 2008

Source: http://politicalhumor.about.com/od/sarahpalin/a/palin-top-10.htm .....interview with Katie Couric, CBS News.

Trent Franks

"FAR more of the African American community is being devastated by the policies of today than were being devastated by policies of slavery."

» What is he: U.S. Congressman
» Where is he from: Arizona
» Date of quote: February 26, 2010

Source: http://yglesias.thinkprogress.org/archives/2010/02/rep-trent-franks-blacks-were-better-off-under-slavery.php

Mike Pence

"WE'RE focused 100% on stopping this government takeover."

»   What is he: U.S.Congressman
»   Where is he from: Indiana
»   Date of quote: April 1, 2010

Source: Fox News http://www.youtube.com/watch?v=w_krcvAANsM

Scott Brown

"AN entire year has gone to waste," "Millions of Americans have lost their jobs, and many more jobs are in danger. Even now, the president still hasn't gotten the message."

» What is he: U. S. Senator
» Where is he from: Massachusetts
» Date of quote: March 13, 2010

Source: http://www.msnbc.msn.com/id/35857741/

Trent Lott

(Williams asked Lott whether he considers homosexuality a sin) "YOU should still love that person. You should not try to mistreat them or treat them as outcasts. You should try to show them a way to deal with that problem, just like alcohol ... or sex addiction ... or kleptomaniacs."

» What is he: Former Speaker of the House
» Where is he from: Mississippi
» Date of quote: June 16, 2002

Source: http://www.skeptictank.org/hs/lott-gay.htm and "The Armstrong Williams Show" on the America's Voice television network.

2nd Source: http://en.wikipedia.org/wiki/Trent_Lott

Condoleezza Rice

"AS I was telling my husb –As I was telling President Bush."

» What is she: Former U.S. Secretary of State
» Where is she from: Texas
» Date of quote: May 3, 2004

Source: Newsweek, May 3, 2004

Eric Cantor

"I think she's living in another world – I really do," Cantor said of the California Democrat House Speaker Nancy Pelosi.

» What is he: House Minority Republican Whip
» Where is he from: Virginia
» Date of quote: September 23, 2009

Source: POLITICOhttp://www.politico.com/news/stories/0909/27461.html

Rush Limbaugh

"NO surprise that the center of the Catholic Church abuse took place in very liberal, or perhaps the nation's most liberal area, Boston."

» What is he: Radio host
» Where is he from: Missouri
» Date of quote: July 21, 2005

Source: http://en.wikipedia.org/wiki/Rick_Santorum

John Fleming

On Health Care Reform "WE should either scrap this bill completely and throw it away and forget about it. Or scrap it and start over again."

» What is he: U.S. Congressman
» Where is he from: Louisiana
» Date of quote: March 17, 2010

Source: http://videocafe.crooksandliars.com/heather/thom-hartmann-im-dizzy-do-republican-alway

Mike Pence

"HOUSE Republicans will not rest until we repeal Obama care lock, stock and barrel and replace it with health care reform that will lower the cost of health insurance without growing the size of government."

- » What is he: U.S.Congressman
- » Where is he from: Indiana
- » Date of quote: April 14, 2010

Source: http://www.politico.com/news/stories/0410/35796.html

Tim Pawlenty

"MR. President, you said 'We don't have any more money as a nation.' Well, if we don't have any money, stop spending it, second of all, stop taxing us into oblivion. Stop spending us into bankruptcy and the next time you have the chance to address the young people of America, maybe you should apologize for dumping this crushing amount of debt on their head and shoulders."

»   What is he: A Governor
»   Where is he from: Minnesota
»   Date of quote: July 15, 2009

Source:http://www.foxbusiness.com/search-results/m/25223740/gov-pawlenty-on-minnesota-s-budget-deficit.htm

2nd Source:http://minnesota.publicradio.org/display/web/2009/10/13/pawlenty-obama-afghanistan-spending/

Condoleezza Rice

"I do not recall being told of anything concerning prisoner abuse."

» What is she: Former U.S. Secretary of State
» Where is she from: Texas
» Date of quote: September 12, 2004

Source: http://www.usatoday.com/news/washington/2004-09-12-rice-denise-abuse_x.htm

Brit Hume

"THERE is no evidence that the United States' use of torture has served as a "recruiting tool" for terrorist groups."

» What is he: Fox News senior political analyst
» Where is he from: Fox Cable News
» Date of quote: April 19, 2009

Source: Broadcasting Co.'s Fox News Sunday

Jon Voight

"DO not let the Obama administration fool you with all their cunning Alinsky methods. And if you don't know what that method is, I implore you to get the book "Rules for Radicals," by Saul Alinsky. Mr. Obama is very well trained in these methods."

» What is he: Actor
» Where is he from: New York
» Date of quote: August 21, 2009

Source; http://www.salon.com/news/politics/war_room/2009/08/21/voight

Saxby Chambliss

"THERE has always been a rush to the polls by African-Americans early," He predicted the crowds of early voters would motivate Republicans to turn out. "It has also got our side energized, they see what is happening."

»   What is he: U.S. Senator
»   Where is he from: Georgia
»   Date of quote: November 14, 2008

Source: http://www.nytimes.com/2008/10/30/us/ politics/30chambliss.html

Tom DeLay

"I don't believe there is a separation of church and state. I think the Constitution is very clear. The only separation is that there will not be a government church."

» What is he: Former House Republican Whip
» Where is he from: Texas
» Date of quote: July 2001

Source: http://en.wikiquote.org/wiki/Tom_DeLay

2nd Source: About.com...At a TV preachers' Congressional luncheon

Rodney Alexander

"THE health care bill we are expected to vote on is a disaster waiting to happen, and an expansion of an already broken program."

» What is he: Governor
» Where is he from: Louisiana
» Date of quote: August 11, 2004

Source: http://thehayride.com/2010/03/alexander-health-care-bill-a-disaster-waiting-to-happen/ MyDD Direct Democracy

Rush Limbaugh

"EXERCISE freaks ... are the ones putting stress on the health care system."

> » What is he: Radio host
> » Where is he from: Missouri
> » Date of quote: June 11, 2009

Source: Rush Limbaugh Show

Dan Burton

"THE American people are vehemently opposed to his radical, left-wing agenda and, for a year now, we've been taking the fight to the administration over their big government, tax and spend policies, and it's a fight we've been winning."

» What is he: U.S Congressman
» Where is he from: Indiana
» Date of quote: January 15, 2010

Source:http://www.facebook.com/notes/danny-burton/burton-responds-to-obamas-war-cry/297526127456

John Boehner

(Referring to the tea party's "Contract from America")
"CAPTURES the American people's frustration with a government that has grown too big, too costly, and too arrogant."

» What is he: GOP House Republican Leader
» Where is he from: Ohio
» Date of quote: April 15, 2010

Source: http://www.politico.com/news/stories/0410/35859.html

Trent Lott

"IT'S time for the president to search the nation to find the best man, woman, or minority to fill the Supreme Court vacancy."

- » What is he: Former Speaker of the House
- » Where is he from: Mississippi
- » Date of quote: October 28, 2005

Source: http://thisblogkillsfascists.blogspot.com/2005/10/best-trent-lott-quote-ever.html.... live on CNN:

Dr. Bill Frist

"THERE just seems to be insufficient information to conclude that Terri Schiavo is [in a] persistent vegetative state. I question it based on a *review of the video footage*, which I spent an hour or so looking at last night in my office here in the Capitol."

»   What is he: Former U.S. Senator
»   Where is he: Tennessee
»   Date of quote: March 17, 2005

Source: http://www.washingtonpost.com/wp-dyn/articles/A48119-2005Mar18.html.... The Washington Post

Rick Perry

"THE hope and change the Democrats had in mind was nothing more than a retread of the failed and discredited socialist policies that have been the enemy of freedom for centuries all over the world. I fear America is teetering towards tyranny."

» What is he: Governor
» Where is he from: Texas
» Date of quote: February 18, 2010

Source: Washington, D.C. –Conservative Political Action Committee (CPAC) 2010 Conference.

Dick Cheney

"THE techniques the Bush administration approved "legal, essential, justified, successful and the right thing to do. President Obama has weakened the country's ability to combat al Qaeda and other extremists by eliminating them."

» What is he: Previous Vice President
» Where is he from: Wyoming
» Date of quote: May 21, 2009

Source: http://www.cnn.com/2009/POLITICS/05/21/cheney.speech/ index.html

Liz Cheney

"THESE "interrogation methods" kept us safe – and that's all the justification they need."

» What is she: Former Deputy Assistant Secretary of State
» Where is she from: Virginia
» Date of quote: May 12, 2009

Source: MSNBC http://crooksandliars.com/david-neiwert/liz-cheney-waterboarding

Michele Bachmann

"AND what a bizarre time we're in, Jan, when a judge will say to little children that you can't say the pledge of allegiance, but you must learn that homosexuality is normal and you should try it."

»   What is she: U.S. Congresswoman
»   Where is she from: Minnesota
»   Date of quote: March 6, 2004

Source:http://www.thebachmannrecord.com/thebachmannrecod. html— Senator Michele Bachmann, appearing as guest on radio program "Prophetic Views Behind The News", hosted by Jan Markell, KKMS 980-AM, March 6, 2004

Newt Gingrich

"I'M not a natural leader. I'm too intellectual; I'm too abstract; I think too much."

» What is he: Former Speaker of the U.S. House of Representatives
» Where is he from: Pennsylvania
» Date of quote: November 9, 2008

Source: http://www.brainyquote.com/quotes/authors/n/newt_gingrich.html

Jon Kyle

"JUDGE Sotomayor rejected the notion that judges should strive for an impartial brand of justice," "She has clearly 'accepted' that her gender and Latina heritage will affect the outcome of her cases."

» What is he: U.S. Senator
» Where is he from: Arizona
» Date of quote: July 13, 2009

Source: http://www.cnsnews.com/public/Content/Article.aspx?rsrcid=50967

Rush Limbaugh

"WE'VE already donated to Haiti. It's called the U.S. income tax. "

» What is he: Radio host
» Where is he from: Missouri
» Date of quote: January 13, 2010

Source: Rush Limbaugh Show—Rush Limbaugh, discouraging
donations to relief efforts in Haiti after the devastating earthquake.

Rand Paul

"WHAT I don't like from the president's administration is this sort of, 'I'll put my boot heel on the throat of BP,'" Paul said. "I think that sounds really un-American in his criticism of business."

» What is he: A Doctor
» Where is he from: Kentucky
» Date of quote: May 28, 2010

Source: http://news.yahoo.com/s/ynews/20100521/pl_ynews/ynews_pl2182 ABC's "Good Morning America"

Janice Kay Brewer

FACT...By enacting the 2011 budget, Brewer and the legislature have eliminated the Arizona variant of the State Children's Health Insurance Program that provides health insurance to uninsured children.

»   What is she: Governor
»   Where is she from: Arizona
»   Date of action: 2010

Source:http://www.democraticunderground.com/discuss/duboard. php?az=view_all&address=389x8205909

Newt Gingrich

(President Obama) "THE most radical president in American history" who oversees a "secular, socialist machine."

» What is he: Former Speaker of the U.S. House of Representatives
» Where is he from: Pennsylvania
» Date of quote: April 8, 2010

Source: Southern Republican Leadership Conference

Sarah Palin

"THE election is only seven months away, Now, when they say, yes we can, we stand up and say, Oh no you don't."

» What is she: Former Governor
» Where is she from: Alaska
» Date of quote: April 8, 2010

Source: Southern Republican Leadership Conference

Mitt Romney

"IN pursuit of a peace process, the United States today has exerted substantial pressure on Israel while putting almost no pressure on the Palestinians and the Arab world. Inexplicably, the United States now places the burden on Israel to make still more unilateral concessions."

- » What is he: Former Governor
- » Where is he from: Massachusetts
- » Date of quote: October 11, 2009

Source: http://www.usnews.com/news/blogs/god-and-country/2009/10/20/

http://img.timeinc.net/time/daily/2009/0902/mitt_romney_0205.jpg

Glenn Beck

PRESIDENT Obama is using Hollywood in an attempt to turn America into a communist nation: "Well, this is fantastic. It's almost like we're living in Mao's China right now."

» What is he: Host, The Glenn Beck Program
» Where is he from: Fox Cable News
» Date of quote: October 10, 2009

Source: http://www.huffingtonpost.com/2009/10/19/glenn-beck-slams-obama-en_n_326632.html

2nd Source: http://mediamatters.org/research/200910200046

Don Rumsfeld

"AS you know, you go to war with the army you have, not the army you might want or wish to have at a later time."

» What is he: Former U.S. Secretary of Defense
» Where is he from: Texas
» Date of quote: December 12, 2004

Source: CNN, 2004-12-08. URL accessed on 2006-04-07. Responding to the question "Why do we soldiers have to dig through local landfills for pieces of scrap metal and compromised ballistic glass to up-armor our vehicles?"

Karl Rove

"THEY are going to exact their revenge this fall and it's not going to be pretty for Democrats."

» What is he: President George W. Bush's chief strategist
» Where is he from: Colorado
» Date of quote: March 14, 2010

Source: NBC's Meet the Press

Barbara Bush

"WHAT I'm hearing which is sort of scary is that they all want to stay in Texas. Everybody is so overwhelmed by the hospitality. And so many of the people in the arena here, you know, were underprivileged anyway so this (chuckle) – this is working very well for them."

» What is she: Former First Lady
» Where is she from: New York
» Date of quote: September 5, 2005

Source: Former First Lady Barbara Bush, on the hurricane evacuees at the Astrodome in HoustonSource:http://politicalhumor.about.com/gi/o.htm?zi=1/XJ&zTi=1&sdn=politicalhumor&cdn=entertainment&tm=42&gps=346_512_1280_575&f=22&su=p504.3.336.ip_&tt=2&bt=0&bts=0&st=23&zu=http%3A//www.editorandpublisher.com/eandp/news/article_display.jsp%3Fvnu_content_id%3D1001054719

Michael C. Burgess

"I don't think that you should be fired," (Geithner) "I thought you should have never been hired."

» What is he: U.S Congressman
» Where is he from: Texas
» Date of quote: November 19, 2009

Source:http://www.cbsnews.com/stories/2009/11/20/politics/
washingtonpost/main5722240.shtml

Ted Nugent

"OBAMA, he's a piece of shit. I told him to suck on my machine gun. Hey Hillary." "You might want to ride one of these into the sunset, you worthless bitch."

» What is he: Singer
» Where is he from: Michigan
» Date of quote: August 22, 2007

Source: http://en.wikipedia.org/wiki/Ted_Nugent

2nd Source: ttp://www.liveleak.com/view?i=9a1_1250550290

3rd Source: http://www.arrested.com/mugs/ted_nugent.html

Sam Brownback

"I want to be the president to appoint the Justice who is the final vote that we need to overturn Roe v. Wade, and end this night of wrong."

» What is he: U.S. Senator
» Where is he from: Kansas
» Date of quote: September 17, 2007

Source: 2007 GOP Values Voter Presidential Debate Sep 17, 2007

http://www.ontheissues.org/social/Sam_Brownback_Abortion.htm

Anthony Robert Martin-Trigona AKA Andy Martin

"A crooked, slimy Jew who has a history of lying and thieving common to members of his race."

» What is he: 2010 Republican candidate for U.S. Senator
» Where is he from: Connecticut
» Date of quote: 1983

Source: http://en.wikipedia.org/wiki/Andy_Martin_(U.S._politician) in reference to a 1983 bankruptcy case, Martin called the judge.

Trent Franks

"I feel this may not only be unconstitutional, but it is unconscionable," "When we start seeing these types of socialist tendencies (mandated health insurance and the pending cap and trade bill), people should become very concerned."

» What is he: U.S. Congressman
» Where is he from: Arizona
» Date of quote: April 10, 2010

Source:http://kingmandailyminer.com/main.asp?SectionID=1&SubSectionID=1&ArticleID=37343&TM=39375.94 U.S. Rep. Trent Franks speaks in a town hall meeting at Kingman First Assembly of God Church Saturday.

Rush Limbaugh

"HE is exaggerating the effects of the disease. He's moving all around and shaking and it's purely an act. This is really shameless of Michael J. Fox. Either he didn't take his medication or he's acting."

» What is he: Radio host
» Where is he from: Missouri
» Date of quote: October 23, 2006

Source: Rush Limbaugh Show – on an ad by Michael J. Fox endorsing Claire McCaskill for Senate for supporting embryonic stem cell research.

Dr. Tom Coburn

"LESBIANISM is so rampant in some of the schools in southeast Oklahoma that they'll only let one girl go to the bathroom. Now think about it. Think about that issue. How is it that that's happened to us?"

» What is he: U.S. Senator
» Where is he from: Oklahoma
» Date of quote: August 31, 2004

Source: Wikiquote: GOP Senate candidate in Oklahoma speaks of 'rampant' lesbianism in schools

Newt Gingrich

"THE more successful they've been at intercepting and stopping bad guys, the less proof there is that we're in danger. And therefore, the better they've done at making sure there isn't an attack, the easier it is to say, 'Well, there never was going to be an attack anyway.' And it's almost like they should every once in a while have allowed an attack to get through just to remind us."

- » What is he: Former Speaker of the U.S. House of Representatives
- » Where is he from: Pennsylvania
- » Date of quote: May 29, 2008

Source: Claremont Colleges http://rawstory.com/news/2008/ Gingrich_Bush_should_have_allowed_attack_0529.html

John Boehner

"THEY got everything else in the entire bureaucracy that they need to control our health care system is all in place with the signing of this bill. That's why *repealing* this bill has to be our number one priority."

» What is he: GOP House Republican Leader
» Where is he from: Ohio
» Date of quote: April 12, 2010

Source: politico.com...The Bud Hedinger Show

Kirk Dillard

"IF I wanted to be part of socialized medicine, I would have moved to Europe. I'll be damned if I'm going to let a socialistic Washington shove a new mandate down the taxpayers' throats of Illinois, especially if it's health care."

» What is he: U.S. Senator
» Where is he from: Illinois
» Date of quote: November 5, 2009

Source: http://newsblogs.chicagotribune.com/clout_st/2009/11/
republican-governor-candidates-bash-the-democrats.html

Rudy Giuliani

"PRESIDENT Obama thinks we can all hold hands, sing songs, and have peace symbols ... North Korea and Iran are not singing along with the president. Knowing that, it just doesn't make sense why we would reduce our nuclear arms when we face these threats."

» What is he: 2008 Republican presidential candidate
» Where is he from: New York
» Date of quote: April 6, 2010

Source: : http://www.sodahead.com/united-states/ronald-reagan-was-a-peacenik-like-obama/blog-297193/

Andre Bauer

"CAN show you a bar graph where free and reduced lunch has the worst test scores in the state of South Carolina."

- » What is he: Lt. Governor
- » Where is he from: South Carolina
- » Date of quote: January 23, 2010

Source; http://www.thestate.com/2010/01/23/1123844/bauer-needy-owe-something-back.html

2nd Source: http://www.informationclearinghouse.info/article24499.htm

Rand Paul

"WE'RE the only country I know that allows people to come in illegally, have a baby, and then that baby becomes a citizen," Paul told RT, a Russian news channel. "And I think that that should stop also."

» What is he: A Doctor
» Where is he from: Kentucky
» Date of quote: May 28, 2010

Source: http://tpmlivewire.talkingpointsmemo.com/2010/05/ rand-paul-children-of-illegal-immigrants-should-not-be-us-citizens-video.php

Lamar Alexander

"LET'S start over, and urge the president not to try to jam his own measure through Congress and a Republican wall of opposition. It's not appropriate."

» What is he: Senator
» Where is he from: Tennessee
» Date of quote: February 25, 2010

Source: WASHINGTON, (Reuters) at Healthcare Summit

Zell Miller

"HE (President Obama) should quit gallivanting all around the globe and fix problems in the U.S."

» What is he: Former U.S Senator
» Where is he from: Georgia
» Date of quote: July 16, 2009

Source: http://www.gpb.org/news/2009/07/16/zell-miller-lashes-out-at-obama-administration

Trent Franks

"OBAMA'S first act as president of any consequence, in the middle of a financial meltdown, was to send taxpayers' money overseas to pay for the killing of unborn children in other countries. Now, I got to tell you, if a president will do that, there's almost nothing that you should be surprised at after that. We shouldn't be shocked that he does all these other insane things. A president that has lost his way that badly, that has no ability to see the image of God in these little fellow human beings, if he can't do that right, then he has no place in any station of government and we need to realize that *he is an enemy of humanity.*"

» What is he: U.S. Congressman
» Where is he from: Arkansas
» Date of quote: September 29, 2009

Source:http://www.cbsnews.com/blogs/2009/09/29/politics/ politicalhotsheet/entry5350756.shtml

Karl Rove

"AS people do better, they start voting like Republicans – unless they have too much education and vote Democratic, which proves there can be too much of a good thing."

» What is he: President George W. Bush's chief strategist
» Where is he from: Colorado
» Date of quote: October 2006

Source: Republican social gathering http://urbanlegends.about.com/ library/bl_bush_on_voting_republican.htm

John McCain

"CARTER has earned his place, if not the worst President in history certainly the worst President of the 20th Century."

- » What is he: U.S. Senator
- » Where is he from: Arizona
- » Date of quote: September 17, 2009

Source: http://www.youtube.com/watch?v=H-LhzEhEbVU&feature=player_embedded

Don Rumsfeld

"I'm not into this detail stuff. I'm more concepty."

"I don't do quagmires."

"I don't do diplomacy."

"I don't do foreign policy."

"I don't do predictions."

"I don't do numbers."

"I don't do book reviews."

» What is he: Former U.S. Secretary of Defense
» Where is he from: Texas
» Date of quote: 2002

Source: http://www.rightwingnews.com/quotes/rummyquotes.php

Dick Cheney

"IN my long experience in Washington, few matters have inspired so much contrived indignation and phony moralizing as the interrogation methods applied to a few captured terrorists."

» What is he: Previous Vice President
» Where is he from: Wyoming
» Date of quote: May 21, 2009

Source: http://www.cnn.com/2009/POLITICS/05/21/cheney.speech/index.html

Sarah Palin

"BACK off his reckless plan to close Guantanamo, begin treating terrorists as wartime enemies, not suspects alleged to have committed crimes, and recognize that the real nature of the terrorist threat requires a commander-in-chief, not a constitutional law professor."

» What is she: Former Governor
» Where is she from: Alaska
» Date of quote: January 5, 2010

Source: http://www.examiner.com/x-30890-Sarah-Palin-Examiner~y2010m1d6-Palin-Obamas-approach-to-terrorism-fatally-flawed

Mike Pence

(Referring to the tea party's "Contract from America") "AS Republicans move forward developing our agenda for the 112th Congress, efforts like this will be invaluable."

» What is he: U.S. Congressman
» Where is he from: Indiana
» Date of quote: April 15, 2010

Source: http://www.politico.com/news/stories/0410/35859.html

Janice Kay Brewer

"GREAT relief, to say the least, to get out of that *hellhole* in Phoenix."

» What is she: Governor
» Where is she from: Arizona
» Date of quote: August 21, 2009

Source: http://www.politico.com/news/stories/0410/36258.html#ixzz0ly2GcSsY

Ben Stein

"[OBAMA] understands nothing. He wants to shut down the oil companies, take away their profits. Kill every state teacher's pension fund that's invested in XOM [Exxon Mobil]. I am terrified of this guy. Either somebody has got to wise him up or he has to wise up himself or he will be real dangerous."

» What is he: Actor, Writer, Lawyer
» Where is he from: Washington D.C.
» Date of quote: February 14, 2008

Source: http://blogsforvictory.com/2008/02/15/ben-stein-obama-will-be-real-dangerous/ Kudlow & Company.

Michael Steele

"OUR platform is one of the best political documents that's been written in the last 25 years. Honest Injun on that."

» What is he: Republican National Committee Chairman
» Where is he from: Maryland
» Date of quote: January 4, 2010

Source: Fox News& http://thinkprogress.org/2010/01/05/steele-injun/

Mike Huckabee

"HOW would the government of the United States feel if Prime Minister Netanyahu began to dictate which people could live in the Bronx, which ones could live in Manhattan, which ones could live in Queens, and say, you know, we only allow certain people to live in these neighborhoods. Jews should be allowed to build in their own land."

»   What is he: Former Governor
»   Where is he from: Arkansas
»   Date of quote: August 18, 2009

Source: http://www.cbsnews.com/blogs/2009/08/18/world/worldwatch/entry5248711.shtml

Chris Smith

"OBAMA recognizes this political reality and is seeking 'pull one over' on the American public saying that his plan won't fund abortion."

» What is he: U.S. Congressman
» Where is he from: Louisiana
» Date of quote: September 10, 2009

Source: http://topics.treehugger.com/quote/0aJCeJo4ZQ9KS?q=Chris+ Smith

Dick Cheney

"GO f*ck yourself." (to Sen. Patrick Leahy)

» What is he: Previous Vice President
» Where is he from: Wyoming
» Date of quote: June 25, 2004

Source: http://politicalhumor.about.com/b/2004/06/25/cheney-to-leahy-go-fk-yourself.htm During an angry exchange on the Senate floor about profiteering by Halliburton

Scott Brown

"SOMEHOW, the greater the public opposition to the health care bill, the more determined they seem to force it on us anyway."

- » What is he: U. S. Senator
- » Where is he from: Massachusetts
- » Date of quote: March 13, 2010

Source: http://www.msnbc.msn.com/id/35857741/..Wall Street Journal

Dr. Jack Cassell

"IF you voted for Obama, seek urologic care elsewhere. Changes to your healthcare begin right now, not in four years."

» What is he: Urologist
» Where is he from: Florida
» Date of posting: March 31, 2010

Source: http://articles.orlandosentinel.com/2010-04-02/news/ os-mount-dora-doctor-tells-patients-go-aw20100401_1_health-care-doctor-patients

Michele Bachmann

"SPENDING comes just as natural to liberals in Minnesota and the Minnesota legislature as bashing decency comes to the editorial board of our major metropolitan newspapers."

- » What is she: U.S. Congresswoman
- » Where is she from: Minnesota
- » Date of quote: October 10-11, 2003

Source: http://en.wikiquote.org/wiki/Michele_Bachmann

Picture Source: http://www.onepennysheet.com

Randy Neugebauer

"IT'S a baby killer."

» What is he :U.S. Congressman
» Where is he from: Texas
» Date of quote; March 19, 2010

Source: http://news.yahoo.com/s/ap/20100322/ap_on_go_co/us_health_overhaul_baby_killer

Picture Source: http://www.michaelmoore.com/words/latest-news/rep-randy-neugebauer-i-yelled-baby-killer-during-rep-bart-stupaks-speech

Newt Gingrich

"THE idea that a congressman would be tainted by accepting money from private industry or private sources is essentially a socialist argument."

»   What is he: Former Speaker of the U.S. House of Representatives
»   Where is he from: Pennsylvania
»   Date of quote: Mother Jones October 1989 Issue.

Source: http://www.conservapedia.com/Newt_Gingrich

Picture Source: http://latimesblogs.latimes.com/photos/ uncategorized/2007/06/28/newt.jpg

Saxby Chambliss

"IF gays are allowed to serve openly in the military, it would lead to all sorts of terrible things, including (Alcohol use, adultery, fraternization, and body art). The presence in the armed forces of persons who demonstrate a propensity or intent to engage in homosexual acts would very likely create an unacceptable risk to those high standards."

» What is he: U.S. Senator
» Where is he from: Georgia
» Date of quote: February 2, 1020

Source: http://blogs.ajc.com/cynthia-tucker/2010/02/02/chambliss-if-gays-serve-therell-be-omg-tattoos/?cxntfid=blogs_cynthia_tucker

Picture Source: http://www.esquire.com/cm/esquire/images/saxby-chambliss-1108-lg-52345089.jpg

John Fleming

"NOT surprised that the socialist liberal pro-abortion forces of the Democrat Party are working not only in the United States to advance abortion and the numbers of abortions but also to export that to other countries."

» What is he: U.S. Congressman
» Where is he from: Louisiana
» Date of quote: April 1, 2010

Source: http://www.lifesitenews.com/ldn/2010/apr/10040112.html

2nd Source; http://888webtoday.com/articles/viewnews.cgi?id=EkZpkEpkEVdktgWVrJ

Mitch Daniels

"CALL the state's attorney general to see if we can join one of the lawsuits to overturn ObamaCare. Yes, it's a long shot. But why not try?"

» What is he: Governor
» Where is he from: Indiana
» Date of quote: March 25, 2010

Source: http://online.wsj.com/article/SB20001424052748704896104 575139830588195568.html

Picture Source: http://image3.examiner.com/images/blog/wysiwyg/ image/Mitch_Daniels.jpg

Mike Pence

"WE'RE going to use every means at our disposal to oppose this government takeover of health care."

» What is he: U.S.Congressman
» Where is he from: Indiana
» Date of quote: April 4, 2010

Source:http://mikepence.house.gov/index.php?option=com_blog_ca lendar&year=2010&month=03&day=21&modid=89....CNN Sunday program

Tea Party People

TEA Party in Washington DC.

» What are they: Protesters against the President of the United States of America
» Where are they from: Washington D.C.

Source: http://gawker.com/5518012/teabagger-seems-to-want-someone-to-go-back-to-kenya

Picture via Dave Weigel. (One more from Ana Marie Cox!)

Sarah Palin

"WE used to hustle over the border for health care we received in Canada. And I think now, isn't that ironic?"

» What is she: Former Governor
» Where is she from: Alaska
» Date of quote: March 8, 2010

Source: Medicine Hat News.. http://washingtonindependent. com/78624/palin-growing-up-i-hustled-over-the-border-for-health-care

Picture Source: http://politicolnews.com/wp-content/ uploads/2009/07/SARAH-PALIN-WINK-WINK-2012.jpg

Lindsey Graham

"IF the Obama administration and congressional Democrats go down this path and push a bill on the American people they do not want, it could be the beginning of the end of the Obama presidency."

» What is he: U.S. Senator
» Where is he from: South Carolina
» Date of quote: September 9, 2009

Source: http://www.politico.com/news/stories/0909/26970.html. President Barack Obama. "address to Congress"

Jim DeMint

"THIS health care issue Is D-Day for freedom in America." "If we're able to stop Obama on this it will be his Waterloo. It will break him."

» What is he: U.S. Senator
» Where is he from: South Carolina
» Date of quote: March 17, 2009

Source:http://www.politico.com/blogs/bensmith/0709/Health_ reform_foes_plan_Obamas_Waterloo.html

Picture Source: http://www.topnews.in/files/JIM_DEMINT.jpg

Mike Pence

"I occasionally got called the Rush Limbaugh of Indiana."

» What is he: U.S.Congressman
» Where is he from: Indiana
» Date of quote: March 22, 2005

Source: Washington Post Page A15 *By Christopher Lee*

Mike Huckabee

"UNEXPECTED offstage noise was Democrat Barack Obama looking to avoid a gunman."

> »   What is he: Former Governor
> »   Where is he from: Arkansas
> »   Date of quote: May 16, 2008

Source: The Huffington Post http://rawstory.com/news/2008/ Huckabee_jokes_about_Obama_ducking_gunman_0516.html

Glenn Beck

"THIS president I think has exposed himself over and over again as a guy who has a deep-seated hatred for white people or the white culture....I'm not saying he doesn't like white people, I'm saying he has a problem. This guy is, I believe, a racist."

» What is he: Host, The Glenn Beck Program
» Where is he from: Fox Cable News
» Date of Quote: July 28, 2009

Source: The Glenn Beck Program FOX News show

Jerry Schweighart

(President Obama) "I don't think he's an American, personally."

» What is he: Mayor
» Where is he from: Illinois
» Date of quote: April 16, 2010

Source: http://celebrifi.com/gossip/Illinois-Mayor-Doesnt-Believe-that-Obama-is-American-Sigh-2249182.html

Orrin Hatch

"AND if they get there, of course, you're going to have a very rough time having a two-party system in this country, because almost everybody's going to say, 'All we ever were, all we ever are, all we ever hope to be *depends on the Democratic Party.*" "That's their goal."

» What is he: U.S Senator
» Where is he from: Utah
» Date of quote: November 2, 2009

Source: http://thehill.com/blogs/blog-briefing-room/news/65853-hatch-health-bills-threaten-two-party-system... interview with the conservative CNSNews.com.

Condoleezza Rice

"OH, indeed there is a tie between Iraq and what happened on 9/11. It's not that Saddam Hussein was somehow himself and his regime involved in 9/11, but, if you think about what caused 9/11, it is the rise of ideologies of hatred that lead people to drive airplanes into buildings in New York."

» What is she: Former U.S. Secretary of State
» Where is she from: Texas
» Date of quote: November 28, 2003

Source: CBS News, November 28, 2003

Mike Huckabee

"I have not bashed America! I haven't even bashed Obama's anti-Israel and promise breaking policy, and I have certainly had the opportunity."

» What is he: Former Governor
» Where is he from: Arkansas
» Date of quote: August 19, 2009

Source: Mike Huckabee Facebook

Mitch Daniels

"WE better start adjusting to our new status as good Europeans."

» What is he: Governor
» Where is he from: Indiana
» Date of quote: March 25, 2010

Source: The wall street Journal http://online.wsj.com/article/SB10001 42405274870409410457514436296840864O.html

Mitt Romney

"AMERICA has just witnessed an unconscionable abuse of power. President Obama has betrayed his oath to the nation."

- » What is he: Former Governor
- » Where is he from: Massachusetts
- » Date of quote: March 22, 2010

Source: National Review.. http://corner.nationalreview.com/post/?q=NzgyMz
A1NWUwNjA5OTg2ZTUzMTliYzQyOTM1ZmIzNTI

Newt Gingrich

"SHOOTING three-point shots may be clever, but it doesn't put anybody to work. What we need is a President, not an athlete."

» What is he: Former Speaker of the U.S. House of Representatives
» Where is he from: Pennsylvania
» Date of quote: April 9, 2010

Source: http://spectator.org/blog/2010/04/13/gingrich-responds-to-norah-odo......Southern Republican Leadership Conference

Don Rumsfeld

"THERE are known "knowns." There are things we know that we know. There are known unknowns. That is to say there are things that we now know we don't know. But there are also unknown unknowns. There are things we do not know we don't know."

» What is he: Former U.S. Secretary of Defense
» Where is he from: Texas
» Date of quote: June 6, 2002

Source: Press Conference at NATO Headquarters, Brussels, Belgium

Tom DeLay

"YOU know, there is an argument to be made that these extensions, the unemployment benefits keeps people from going and finding jobs. In fact there are some studies that have been done that show people stay on unemployment compensation and they don't look for a job until two or three weeks before they know the benefits are going to run out."

» What is he: Former House Republican Whip
» Where is he from: Texas
» Date of quote: March 7, 2010

Source: http://www.huffingtonpost.com/2010/03/07/tom-delay-jim-bunning-was_n_489050.html

Rick Perry

FACT... the picture on the right is Ted Nugent at Rick Perry's Inaugural Ball, draped in a confederate flag shirt. Perry danced, on stage.

» What is he: Governor
» Where is he from: Texas
» Date of Inaugural Ball : 2007

Source: http://www.chron.com/disp/story.mpl//4478848.html ....Rick Perry's 2007 Inaugural Ball

Dale Robertson

Tea Party Taking The Next Step.

"WE are setting the tone for taking back America with Liberty Concerts. We are not waiting until the first quarter of the year, we have already begun."

» What is he: President and Founder of the TeaParty.org
» Where is he from: Texas
» Date of quote: February 27, 2009

Source: http://tpmmuckraker.talkingpointsmemo.com/2010/02/warning_tea_party_in_danger

Steve King

"TODAY the work begins to repeal Obamacare and restore the principles of liberty that made America a great nation. The American people must take their country back by methodically eliminating every vestige of creeping socialism, including socialized medicine. The Pelosi Democrats will pay a price for their overreach. This fight is far from over."

» What is he: U.S. Congressman
» Where is he from: Iowa
» Date of quote: March 22, 2010

Source: Steve King Web page :News Room Press Releases

Paul Wolfowitz

"THERE'S a lot of money to pay for this. It doesn't have to be U.S. taxpayer money. And it starts with the assets of the Iraqi people... We are dealing with a country that can really finance its own reconstruction and relatively soon."

» What is he: Former U.S. Deputy Secretary of Defense
» Where is he from: New York
» Date of quote: March 27, 2003

Source: Testimony before the House Appropriations Committee:

Don Rumsfeld

Saddam Hussein greets Donald Rumsfeld in Baghdad in 1983.

"I can't tell you if the use of force in Iraq today will last five days, five weeks or five months, but it won't last any longer than that."

- » What is he: Former U.S. Secretary of Defense
- » Where is he from: Texas
- » Date of quote: November 14, 2002

Source: Radio interview with Steve Croft, Infinity CBS Radio Connect

Liz Cheney

"MR. Obama's method for pushing reset around the world is becoming clearer with each foreign trip. He proclaims moral equivalence between the U.S. and our adversaries, he readily accepts a false historical narrative, and he refuses to stand up against anti-American lies."

» What is she: Former Deputy Assistant Secretary of State
» Where is she from: Virginia
» Date of quote: July 13, 2009

Source: Wall Street Journal op-ed entitled "Obama rewrites the Cold War"

2nd Source: http://online.wsj.com/article/SB124744075427029805.html

Dick Cheney

"I'VE been concerned at the way we've been presented overseas... What I find disturbing is the extent to which he's gone to Europe and seemed to apologize profusely, been to Mexico and seemed to apologize there," said Cheney. "The world out there, both our friends and foes, will be quick to take advantage of that... I don't think we have much to apologize for."

» What is he: Previous Vice President
» Where is he from: Wyoming
» Date of quote: April 20, 2009

Source: http://www.huffingtonpost.com/2009/04/20/cheney-slams-obama-again_n_189268.html

Anthony Robert Martín-Trigona AKA Andy Martín

FACT...Martin filed a lawsuit against the state of Hawaii calling for the public release of Barack Obama's birth certificate and other vital records.

» What is he: 2010 Republican candidate for U.S. Senator
» Where is he from: Connecticut
» Date of lawsuit: October 17, 2008

Source: http://en.wikipedia.org/wiki/Andy_Martin_(U.S._politician)

Sean Hannety

"PRESIDENT Bush did not play golf while this country was at war. He seemed to be far more in touch."

- » What is he: Fox News Host
- » Where is he from: New York
- » Date of quote: March 3, 2010

Source: "Fox News http://mediamatters.org/mmtv/201002040001

http://www.foxnews.com/images/492821/0_61_320_011309_ha_bush_part2_0.jpg

Rodney Alexander

"THERE are members of the Congress who would like nothing more than to take away an individual's Second Amendment right to bear arms."

» What is he: Governor
» Where is he from: Louisiana
» Date of Source: April 8, 2010

Source: http://www.opencongress.org/people/news/400006_Rodney_Alexander

2nd Source: Ouachita Citizen

Mitch McConnell

"AMERICANS can expect Senate Republicans to make a sustained and vigorous case for judicial restraint and the fundamental importance of an even-handed reading of the law." *(In response to Supreme Court Justice John Paul Stevens' announcement to retire earlier)*

» What is he: Senate Minority Leader U.S. Senator
» Where is he from: Kentucky
» Date of quote: April 10, 2010

Source: Daylife Publishers. http://tpmlivewire.talkingpointsmemo. com/2010/04/mcconnell-on-stevens-replacement-gop-to-make-sustained-and-vigorous-case-for-judicial-restraint.php

Rick Santorum

"[The] President, Clinton. . . is once again releasing American military might on a foreign country with an ill-defined objective and no exit strategy. He has yet to tell the Congress how much this operation will cost. And he has not informed our nation's armed forces about how long they will be away from home. These strikes do not make for a sound foreign policy."

»   What is he: Former U.S. Senator
»   Where is he from: Pennsylvania
»   Date of quote: June 18, 2005

Source: Associated Press Interview

Tom DeLay

(DeLay asked three young hurricane evacuees from New Orleans at the Astrodome in Houston)

"NOW tell me the truth boys, is this kind of fun?"

» What is he: Former House Republican Whip
» Where is he from: Texas
» Date of quote: September 9, 2005

Source: http://blogs.chron.com/domeblog/archives/2005/09/delay_to_evacue.html

2nd Source: http://www.rawstory.com/news/2005/DeLay_to_evacuees_Is_this_kind_of_f_0909.html

Mark Sanford

"WE as a party want to hold ourselves to high standards, period."

» What is he: Governor
» Where is he from: South Carolina
» Date of quote: June 25, 2009

Source:http://www.realclearpolitics.com/articles/2009/06/25/the_meaning_of_sanford_and_political_adultery__97169.html Reuters

Rick Perry

"THIS is an administration hell-bent toward taking American towards a socialist country. And we all don't need to be afraid to say that because that's what it is."

» What is he: Governor
» Where is he from: Texas
» Date of quote; November 11, 2009

Source: http://www.politico.com/news/stories/1109/29424.html

Mitch McConnell

FACT: McConnell (on far right) has commitments from every GOP senator to block Democrats' Wall Street bill.

» What is he: Senate Minority Leader U.S. Senator
» Where is he from: Kentucky
» Date of source: April 17, 2010

Source: http://www.politico.com/news/stories/0410/35938.html#ixzz0lOTwLYcj

Trent Lott

Speaking for Sen. Thurmond (R-S.C.) "I want to say this about my state: When Strom Thurmond ran for president, we voted for him. We're proud of it. And if the rest of the country had followed our lead, we wouldn't have had all these problems over all these years, either."

» What is he: Former Speaker of the House
» Where is he from: Mississippi
» Date of quote: December 5, 2002

Source: Published by the Washington Post

Tom DeLay

"EMOTIONAL appeals about working families trying to get by on $4.25 an hour [the minimum wage in 1996] are hard to resist. Fortunately, such families do not exist."

» What is he: Former House Republican Whip
» Where is he from: Texas
» Date of quote: April 23, 1996

Source: Wikiqauote-Congressional Record, H3706….. A debate in Congress on increasing the minimum wage

John Boehner

"OBAMA administration's plan to move some Guantanamo detainees to Illinois shows that the White House "must've forgotten" about the Americans who died on Sept. 11. I think the administration wasn't around for 9/11."

» What is he: GOP House Republican Leader
» Where is he from: Ohio
» Date of quote: December 15, 2009

Source: http://www.nydailynews.com/news/world/2009/12/16/2009-12-16_midwest_burgs_eager_to_take_in_gitmo_thugs.html

Sarah Palin

"IT may be tempting and more comfortable to just keep your head down, plod along, and appease those who demand: 'Sit down and shut up,' but that's the worthless, easy path; that's a quitter's way out." *(Announced her resignation as governor, July 3, 2009)*

> What is she: Former Governor
> Where is she from: Alaska
> Date of source: January 25, 2010

Source: http://cornellsun.com/section/arts/content/2010/01/25/and-palinisms

Michael Steele

"WHAT has President Obama actually accomplished?' It is unfortunate that the president's star power has outshined tireless advocates who have made real achievements working towards peace and human rights," (speaking of Obama's win of the Noble Peace Price.)

» What is he: Republican National Committee Chairman
» Where is he from: Maryland
» Date of quote: October 10, 2009

Source: http://www.business-standard.com/india/news/
obama\s-nobel-democrats-hail-republicans-slam/75656/on

Mike Huckabee

"WHETHER we need to send somebody to Mars, I don't know. But I'll tell you what, if we do, I've got a few suggestions, and maybe Hillary could be on the first rocket."

» What is he: Former Governor
» Where is he from: Arkansas
» Date of quote: November 28, 2007

Source: http://politicalhumor.about.com/od/mikehuckabee/a/huckabeequotes.htm

2nd Source: http://www.marstoday.com/news/viewnews.html?id=1246

Orrín Hatch

"SO that's what we're putting up with. And I might add that he's (Obama) you know, he talks centrist and everything they do is left. And I believe they're – I believe they're actually running this country right into the ground."

- » What is he: U.S Senator
- » Where is he from: Utah
- » Date of quote: April 1, 2010

Source: http://www.foxnews.com/story/0,2933,590302,00.html

Barbara Bush

"CLINTON lied. A man might forget where he parks or where he lives, but he never forgets oral sex, no matter how bad it is."

» What is she: Former First Lady
» Where is she from: New York
» Date of quote: October 22, 2003

Source: Interview on the CNN LARRY KING LIVE

Jon Voight

"THE stimulus didn't work... We're being told what cars we can drive, how much we can make..." Obama has made this [health care] a personal crusade now... As we can see it really is about him. He is arrogant and he's adamant that he's going to get this passed."

» What is he: Actor
» Where is he from: New York
» Date of quote: September 2, 2009

Source: http://www.examiner.com/x-14650-Entertainment-Examiner~y2009m9d2-Jon-Voight-tears-into-Obama-on-Fox-News-calls-President-arrogant

John Barrasso

"AND, now that oil is starting to climb back to $75 per barrel what is the Democratic plan? Wind."

»   What is he: U.S. Senator
»   Where is he from: Wyoming
»   Date of quote: May 24, 2009

Source: http://gatewaypundit.firstthings.com/2009/05/sen-barrasso-blasts-dems-destructive-energy-plan-in-gop-weekly-address/

John Boehner

"WE are about 24 hours from Armageddon"

- » What is he: GOP House Republican Leader
- » Where is he from: Ohio
- » Date of quote: March 22, 2010

Source: John Boehner's website

2nd Source: http://articles.chicagotribune.com/keyword/welfare

Chris Smith

"BUT the truth is that he (Obama) seeks to cover up his intention to use the government-run public plan to send checks from the U.S. treasury to abortionists around the country. And, use government subsidies to pay for health care plans that cover abortion."

- » What is he: U.S. Congressman
- » Where is he from: Louisiana
- » Date of quote: September 10, 2009

Source: http://www.politicalcrossfire.com/forum/viewtopic.
php?t=128977

Sean Hannety

(Obama) "I think he's the most radical president in American history. I think in that sense we've never seen such radicalism."

» What is he: Fox News Host
» Where is he from: New York
» Date of quote: April 1, 2010

Source:http://www.foxnews.com/story/0,2933,590302,00.html Fox News

Dick Cheney

FACT... Former U.S. Vice President Dick Cheney shot Harry Whittington, a 78-year-old Texas attorney, while participating in a quail hunt on a ranch in Kenedy County, Texas. Both Cheney and Whittington call the incident an accident.

The time of the shooting was not stated by Cheney. The other members of the hunting party put the time variously between 1730 hours and 1800 hours.

Harry Whittington suffered a non-fatal "silent" heart attack and atrial fibrillation due to at least one lead-shot pellet lodged in or near his heart.

» What is he: Previous Vice President
» Where is he from: Wyoming
» Date of shooting: February 10 or 11 or 12 or 13 or 14, 2006. No one knows for sure.

Source: http://en.wikipedia.org/wiki/Dick_Cheney_hunting_incident

Mark Sanford

"AT that point I was very careful, everything was paid for in cash and you won't find a credit card record."

» What is he: Governor
» Where is he from: South Carolina
» Date of quote: June 30, 2009

Source: Interview with the Associated Press in his office at the statehouse in Columbia, S.C.,

2nd Source:http://www.opposingviews.com/p/s-c-gov-mark-sanford-admits-he-crossed-line-with-other-women

Joe Lieberman

"IF the House doesn't have the votes to pass the Senate bill on health care reform, then maybe there's an opportunity for a bipartisan group to get together, and there's no question that Lindsey, and I think some other Republicans, might like to be part of that. It would be a smaller bill."

» What is he: U.S. Senator
» Where is he from: Connecticut
» Date of quote: March 10, 2010

Source: *The Politico dyn.politico.com/printstory.cfm?uuid=45C8B53A-18FE-70B2*

Mike Pence

"THE Obama Administration and the Democrat majority in Congress have taken our economy from bad to worse, with their failed economic agenda and big government plans."

- » What is he: U.S. Congressman
- » Where is he from: Indiana
- » Date of quote: November 27, 2009

Source: http://hotairpundit.blogspot.com/2009/11/gop-weekly-address-congressman-mike.html

Zell Miller

"TODAY we're spending like we're Paris Hilton, regulating like we're Ralph Nader, nationalizing like we're Hugo Chavez, printing money like we're the Weimar Republic."

- » What is he: Former U.S Senator
- » Where is he from: Georgia
- » Date of quote: July 16, 2009

Source: http://www.gpb.org/news/2009/07/16/zell-miller-lashes-out-at-obama-administration

Rush Limbaugh

"ADOLF Hitler, like Barack Obama, also ruled by dictate."

- » What is he: Radio host
- » Where is he from: Missouri
- » Date of quote: August 6, 2009

Source: http://mediamatters.org/mmtv/200908060021:

http://blog.cleveland.com/nationworld_impact/2009/03/large_Rush-Limbaugh-headshot-finger-Jan13-09.jpg

Dan Burton

"WILL NØbama spouting moralism from his Middle East pulpit inspire Muslims to stop their jihad of US and shout for the destruction of Israel? What a good and patient friend they have in Barack Hussein NØbama!"

» What is he: U.S Congressman
» Where is he from: Indiana
» Date of quote: June 4, 2009

Source: http://smalltalkwitht.blogspot.com/2009/06/rep-dan-burton-responds-to-obamas.html....Interview, Fox News

J.D. Hayworth

(When asked about the ongoing wars in Iraq and Afghanistan, which were not declared) "THAT if we want to be sticklers, the war that Dwight Eisenhower led in Europe against the Third Reich *was never declared by the United States Congress.*"

» What is he: Former U.S Congressman
» Where is he from: Arizona
» Date of Source: May 24, 2010

Source: Read more: http://www.politico.com/news/
stories/0510/37701.html#ixzz0pLn8feib

Karen Hughes

"I think that happened *before President Bush left office* when they took the action that they did on TARP and the banks have now repaid much of that money but that's what stabilized the economy and prevented the collapse of the financial system."

- » What is she: Former Under Secretary of State
- » Where is she from: Texas
- » Date of quote: January 17, 2010

Source: NBC Sunday….. in response to journalist Mark Halperin, who praised the current president's handling of the economy.

Joe Lieberman

"I feel so strongly about the creation of another government health insurance entitlement, The government going into the health insurance business – I think it's such a mistake that I would use the power I have as a single senator to stop a final vote."

» What is he: U.S. Senator
» Where is he from: Connecticut
» Date of quote: November 1, 2009

Source: *CBS FACE THE NATION http://thehill.com/homenews/ senate/65765-lieberman-doing-nothing-on-healthcare-better-than- public-option*

Rudy Giuliani

"WE had no domestic attacks under Bush. We've had one under Obama."

» What is he: 2008 Republican presidential candidate
» Where is he from: New York
» Date of quote: January 8, 2010

Source:http://www.washingtonpost.com/wp-srv/nation/specials/
attacked/transcripts/giulianitext_100101.html

Rick Santorum

"I have no problem with homosexuality. I have a problem with homosexual acts."

» What is he: Former U.S. Senator
» Where is he from: Pennsylvania
» Date of quote: April 7, 2003

Source: Associated Press Interview

http://www.catholicvoteaction.org/blog/cva/index.php?p=1295

Mitch McConnell

"THE country really didn't have any serious debt problems until that reckless Obama came to town."

» What is he: Senate Minority Leader U.S. Senator
» Where is he from: Kentucky
» Date of quote: December 27, 2009

Source: Blue Texan Sunday.. http://firedoglake.com/2009/12/27/
mitch-mcconnell-republicans-arent-responsible-for-record-deficit/

Lindsey Graham

"THE American public was tiring of the "crap" and "spin" offered by the Obama administration in an effort to get health care."

> » What is he: U.S. Senator
> » Where is he from: South Carolina
> » Date of quote: March 14, 2010

Source: http://www.huffingtonpost.com/2010/03/14/lindsey-graham-on-obama-h_n_498301.html

Darrell Issa

(Federal government) "JUST threw" buckets of cash at New York for the September 11, 2001 attacks "that had no dirty bomb in it, it had no chemical munitions in it." He went on: "I have to ask ... why the firefighters who went there and everybody in the city of New York needs to come to the federal government for the dollars versus this being primarily a state consideration."

» What is he: U.S. Congressman
» Where is he from: California
» Date of quote: April 2008

Source: http://en.wikipedia.org/wiki/Darrell_Issa#Blackwater_
controversy

Brit Hume

"BUDDHISM is inferior to Christianity when it comes to forgiveness of sins. Tiger Woods should turn his back on Buddhism and become a Christian to be forgiven for cheating on his wife."

»   What is he: Fox News senior political analyst
»   Where is he from: Fox Cable News
»   Date of quote: January 3, 2010

Source: Hume told Fox News' Chris Wallace Sunday

John McCain

OBAMA "IS leading an extreme, left wing crusade to bankrupt America. I stand in his way every day."

» What is he: U.S. Senator
» Where is he from: Arizona
» Date of quote: January 7, 2010

Source:http://blogs.cqpolitics.com/eyeon2010/2010/01/mccain-bashes-obama-in-new-rad.html 2ndSource:http://www.swamppolitics.com/news/politics/blog/2010/01/mccain_vs_obamas_leftwing_crus.html

Laura Bush

FACT...In 1963, according to a public police report, Laura Bush (then known as Laura Welch) was involved in a fatal car accident. According to the report, Laura Welch allegedly had been driving when her car passed a stop sign and struck a sedan driven by 17-year-old named Michael Douglas. No charges were filed as a result of the accident. There was another female teenage passenger in Laura Welch's car. Michael Douglas died after suffering a broken neck.

» What is she: Former First Lady
» Where is she from: Texas
» Date of accident: 1963

Source: public police report ...Highpundits.com

John Boehner

"DEMOCRATS have tried every trick in the book, from attempting to buy off Republicans with pork or intimidate them with polls or call them the "Party of No"– he reiterated, "None of it worked."

»   What is he: GOP House Republican Leader
»   Where is he from: Ohio
»   Date of quote: October 22, 2009

Source: http://firstread.msnbc.msn.com/
archive/2010/02/18/2206185.aspx

Dick Cheney

"MR. Obama's decision to abandon plans to place a missile defense program in Poland and the Czech Republic a blunder and a breach of good faith."

» What is he: Previous Vice President
» Where is he from: Wyoming
» Date of quote: October 22, 2009

Source: http://thecaucus.blogs.nytimes.com/2009/10/22/cheney-slams-obama-on-afghanistan-policy/

Bobby Jindal

"WE don't want to be labeled the party of "no." As it pertains to this bill, how about "hell no"?

» What is he: Governor
» Where is he from: Louisiana
» Date of quote: March 26, 2010

Source:http://online.wsj.com/article/SB10001424052748704094104
575144361145435600.html?KEYWORDS=Bobby+Jindal

Glenn Beck

"YOU got to have an enemy to fight. And when you have an enemy to fight, then you can unite the entire world behind you, and you seize power. That was Hitler's plan. His enemy: the Jew. Al Gore's enemy, the U.N.'s enemy: global warming. Then you get the scientists – eugenics. You get the scientists – global warming. Then you have to discredit the scientists who say, 'That's not right.' And you must silence all dissenting voices. That's what Hitler did."

» What is he: Host, The Glenn Beck Program
» Where is he from: Fox Cable News
» Date of quote: April 30, 2007

Source: Broadcast of The Glenn Beck Program

Tim Pawlenty

"SHE said enough. She said no more. I think we should take a page out of her book. We should take a 9 iron and smash the window out of big government in this country."

» What is he: Governor
» Where is he from: Minnesota
» Date of quote: February 19, 2010

Source: Breibart.tv (What the right can learn from Elin Nordegren, wife of cheating golfer Tiger Woods.

Lindsey Graham

"NOT one Republican will vote for the reconciliation part of this," he said. "Not one Republican voted for the Senate (healthcare) bill. And you are dealing with one-sixth of the economy."

» What is he: U.S. Senator
» Where is he from: South Carolina
» Date of quote: March 7, 2010

Source: http://www.cbsnews.com/stories/2010/03/07/ftn/main6275271.shtml

Sean Hannety

"HE honors the national day of prayer behind closed doors. Now, on his Middle East apology tour, the President calls the U.S. a "Muslim nation."

» What is he: Fox News Host
» Where is he from: New York
» Date of quote: June 5, 2009

Source: Fox News

Karl Rove

On Wall Street Reform, "START over please, Mr. President."

» What is he: President George W. Bush's chief strategist
» Where is he from: Colorado
» Date of quote: April 19, 2010

Source: http://videocafe.crooksandliars.com/heather/thom-hartmann-im-dizzy-do-republican-alway– Fox News' Steve Doocy, Karl Rove, 4/19/10

Mitch McConnell

On Health Care Reform, "HOW much longer do Americans have to wait before Democrat leaders will give up this partisan quest and agree to start over?"

» What is he: Senate Minority Leader U.S. Senator
» Where is he from: Kentucky
» Date of quote: March 10, 2010

Source: http://videocafe.crooksandliars.com/heather/thom-hartmann-im-dizzy-do-republican-alway

2nd Source:http://mcconnell.senate.gov/public/index.cfm?p=PressReleases&ContentRecord_id=4311185d-c405-4a19-af3c-1e6b9b99ca36&ContentType_id=c19bc7a5-2bb9-4a73-b2ab-3c1b5191a72b&Group_id=0fd6ddca-6a05-4b26-8710-a0b7b59a8f1f

Rudy Giuliani

"OH, you dirty boy! Donald, I thought you were a gentleman." – while dressed in drag, after having his "breasts" fondled by Donald Trump.

» What is he: 2008 Republican presidential candidate
» Where is he from: New York
» Date of quote: March 11, 2000

Source: 2000 Mayor's Inner Circle Press Roast

Michael C. Burgess

"THE same Members of Congress who are sent to Washington by the voters in their districts to represent their best interests, told the American people 'we don't care what you want, we don't care what you need, we are going to pass a health bill which you oppose anyway.' Democrats said, 'forget what's best for the country, forget bipartisanship' – the only thing bipartisan about this bill is its opposition."

» What is he: U.S Congressman
» Where is he from: Texas
» Date of quote: March 24, 2010

Source: http://www.thenewsconnection.com/article. cfm?articleID=33360 Congressman Michael C. Burgess, M.D. (R-Texas), Chairman of the Congressional Health Care Caucus, released the following statement after House passage of the Senate health care reform bill on Sunday evening:

Joe Wilson

"You lie"

» What is he: U.S. Congressman
» Where is he from: South Carolina
» Date of quote: January 27, 2010

Source: President Obama's State of the Union Address 2010

Rand Paul

"A message that is loud and clear and does not mince words: We have come to take our government back."

» What is he: A Doctor
» Where is he from: Kentucky
» Date of quote: May 18, 2010

Source: Read more: http://www.time.com/time/nation/article/0,8599,1990183,00.html#ixzz0pMgCJ6ub

Mitch McConnell

"WE must not pass the financial reform bill that's about to hit the floor ... The fact is, this bill wouldn't solve the problems that led to the financial crisis. It would make them worse."

» What is he: Senate Minority Leader U.S. Senator
» Where is he from: Kentucky
» Date of quote: April 13, 2010

Source: Atlanta Journal Constitution Vendor

John McCain

"THE fundamentals of our economy are strong."

(On 'Black Monday', September 15, 2008, when there was a global stock market crash after Lehman Brothers filed for bankruptcy protection and Merrill Lynch agreed to sell itself to Bank of America)

» What is he: U.S. Senator
» Where is he from: Arizona
» Date of quote: September 15, 2008

Source: http://www.huffingtonpost.com/2008/09/15/mccain-fundamentals-of-th_n_126445.html

Tom DeLay

"A woman can take care of the family. It takes a man to provide structure. To provide stability. Not that a woman can't provide stability, I'm not saying that... It does take a father, though."

- » What is he: Former House Republican Whip
- » Where is he from: Texas
- » Date of quote: February 10, 2004

Source: Radio interview...http://en.wikiquote.org/wiki/Tom_DeLay#Women.2Ffamily

Mike Huckabee

"IT is now difficult to keep track of the vast array of publicly endorsed and institutionally supported aberrations—from homosexuality and pedophilia to sadomasochism and necrophilia."

» What is he: Former Governor
» Where is he from: Arkansas
» Date of quote: 1998

Source: Mike Huckabee 1998 book, Kids Who Kill,

Karen Hughes

"THIS president (Bush) has delivered on his promises, and is doing in office what he said he would do, and I think many liberals are just shocked by that."

» What is she: Former Under Secretary of State
» Where is she from: Texas
» Date of quotes: 1994 – 2009

Source: http://www.icelebz.com/quotes/karen_hughes/

Orrin Hatch

"DEMOCRATS are "diabolical" in their pursuit of health reform."

»   What is he: U.S Senator
»   Where is he from: Utah
»   Date of quote: November 2, 2009

Source: http://thehill.com/blogs/blog-briefing-room/news/65853-hatch-health-bills-threaten-two-party-system

Mitch Daniels

"IT'S become clear that the Pelosi bill has little to do with a cooler planet and everything to do with raising money for the out-of-control federal spending now underway in Washington. Please excuse us Midwesterners for feeling a bit like the targets of an imperialistic policy."

» What is he: Governor
» Where is he from: Indiana
» Date of quote: May 30, 2009

Source: http://www.allheadlinenews.com/articles/7015326801

Rick Perry

(Obama) "I think he has socialist beliefs."

» What is he: Governor
» Where is he from: Texas
» Date of source: March 2, 2010

Source: http://www.politico.com/news/stories/0310/33741.html

Michael Steele

On the stimulus package…"IS just a wish list from a lot of people who have been on the sidelines for years, to get a little bling, bling."

» What is he: Republican National Committee Chairman
» Where is he from: Maryland
» Date of quote: March 15, 2009

Source: http://www.huffingtonpost.com/2009/02/09/steele-obama-stimulus-is_n_165295.html

Lamar Alexander

"WE do all the appropriating. They do not do any of it down at the White House. They send a budget up here, and we don't have to pay any attention it to at all. We do what we want to do."

» What is he: Senator
» Where is he from: Tennessee
» Date of quote: March 14, 2005

Source: C-Span.org

2nd Source: http://www.brainyquote.com/quotes/authors/l/lamar_alexander.html

Meg Whitman

FACT...Goldman Sachs paid Whitman $475,000 for her board service, but she left in 2002 after questions were raised about whether Goldman gave her preferential access to stocks that were flipped quickly for huge profits in exchange for eBay Inc.'s investment banking business.

» What is she: Former President and C.E.O. of eBay
» Where is she from: California
» Date of Source: October 5, 2009

Source: http://www.huffingtonpost.com/2010/04/27/whitman-defends-tenure-at_n_554116.html

Rick Santorum

In response to a question, how to prevent sexual abuse of children by priests, "The priests were engaged in "a basic homosexual relationship" with "post-pubescent men."

» What is he: Former U.S. Senator
» Where is he from: Pennsylvania
» Date of quote: April 20, 2009

Source: http://en.wikipedia.org/wiki/Rick_Santorum...Interview with the Associated Press

Eric Cantor

"WHAT the president and the administration did was, they mis-wrote the stimulus bill and got the stimulus wrong. We now find ourselves in a place that the administration promised we wouldn't be."

» What is he: House Minority Republican Whip
» Where is he from: Virginia
» Date of quote; July 5, 2009

Source: http://www.politicsdaily.com

Tim Pawlenty

"He went around the country last fall promising 'change we can believe in,' but now we see it's about changing what we believe in."

» What is he: A Governor
» Where is he from: Minnesota
» Date of quote: August 17, 2009

Source: http://www.politico.com/news/stories/0809/26138.html

Mitt Romney

"I take issue with President Obama's recent tour of apology. It's not because America hasn't made mistakes – we have – but because America's mistakes are overwhelmed by what America has meant to the hopes and aspirations of people throughout the world."

» What is he: Former Governor
» Where is he from: Massachusetts
» Date of quote: June 1, 2009

Source: http://www.allheadlinenews.com/articles/7015326801

Photo: http://courtneyphillips.files.wordpress.com/2007/08/osama-obama-and-chelseas-moma-sign-mitt-romney.jpg

Orrin Hatch

"I'VE never seen it this bad nor have I ever seen a group that is so arrogant that we have in Washington right now. It's absolutely arrogant. They're actually Europeanizing America against our will. They're taking over banks, they're taking over car companies. They're taking over a number of other entities in our society. And basically federalizing everything."

» What is he: U.S Senator
» Where is he from: Utah
» Date of quote: April 1, 2010

Source: http://www.foxnews.com/story/0,2933,590302,00.html

Meg Whitman

Whitman's explanation for her poor voting record. "I was focused on raising a family, on my husband's career, and we moved many, many times."

»   What is she: Former President and C.E.O. of eBay
»   Where is she from: California
»   Date of Source: October 5, 2009

Source: **http://californiaaccountability.com/meg-whitman?utm_ source=google&utm_medium=cpc&utm_content=mw&utm_ campaign=key&gclid=CNDJkNOa-KECFR5OgwodOnELDg** *Contra Costa Times editorial*, **October 5, 2009**

John Boehner

"WASHINGTON Democrats "made history" by imposing a job-killing government takeover of health care on the American people – against their will. Their health care bill will raise taxes, cut Medicare, impose unfunded mandates on the states and, for the first time in more than 30 years, allow public funding of abortions."

» What is he: GOP House Republican Leader
» Where is he from: Ohio
» Date of quote: March 22, 2010

Source:http://republicanleader.house.gov/News/DocumentSingle.aspx?DocumentID=177648

Scott Brown

"MR. President, unfortunately in this economy, not everybody can buy a truck."

» What is he: U. S. Senator
» Where is he from: Massachusetts
» Date of quote: January 16, 2010

Source:http://campaignspot.nationalreview.com/post/?q=ZTM2MmJk MTRlMWE5MTBhODEyZjI2YzEwMDQ2MWIzNmE=

Condoleezza Rice

"I believe that the title was, Bin Laden Determined to Attack inside the United States."

» What is she: Former U.S. Secretary of State
» Where is she from: Texas
» Date of quote: May 13, 2004

Source: http://dearprime.blogspot.com/2006/10/my-favourite-condi-rice-quotes-of-all.html

Lamar Alexander

"The Obama administration's motto," he said, "is turning out to be: 'If we can find it in the Yellow Pages, the government ought to try to do it.'"

» What is he: Senator
» Where is he from: Tennessee
» Date of quote: March 30, 2010

Source:http://www.nytimes.com/2010/03/31/us/politics/31obama.html?scp=4&sq=lamar%20alexander&st=cse

Philip J. Berg

Not one picture to be found, except for the ones that said, "subject to copyright." My son and I are afraid of this man, so, NO PICTURE.

"I am proceeding for the 305 + million people in 'our' U.S.A., for 'our' forefathers and for the thousands and thousands that have died defending our Constitution with the legal fight to prove that Obama is not constitutionally qualified to be President."

» What is he: Lawyer
» Where is he from: Pennsylvania
» Date of quote: January 26, 2009

Source: http://citizenwells.wordpress.com/2009/01/26/philip-j-berg-press-release-january-26-2009-obama-not-eligible-obama-not-natural-born-citizen-berg-has-3-cases-berg-will-prove-obama-ineligible-berg-vs-obama-hollister-vs-soetoro-aka-obama/

Karl Rove

"IT'S a worldwide apology tour, we're sorry, we're wrong and oh incidentally I'm going to bow deeply to the waist to the once divine Japanese Monarchy, I just don't get it, in England they didn't bow, but they bow there. They bowed to the Saudi's, will they bow to the Queen of the Netherlands? Please, get this thing right, I think it is best if American Presidents do what they've always done, which is stand for our small "R" Republican values and do not bow to monarchies."

» What is he: President George W. Bush's chief strategist
» Where is he from: Colorado
» Date of quote: November 16, 2009

Source: http://www.youtube.com/watch?v=_
UdP64CgsDk&feature=player_embedded

Michele Bachmann

"IT isn't that some gay will get some rights. It's that everyone else in our state will lose rights. For instance, parents will lose the right to protect and direct the upbringing of their children. Because our K-12 public school system, of which ninety per cent of all youth are in the public school system, they will be required to learn that homosexuality is normal, equal and perhaps you should try it. And that will occur immediately, that all schools will begin teaching homosexuality."

»   What is she: U.S. Congresswoman
»   Where is she from: Minnesota
»   Date of quote: March 6, 2004

Source: Guest on radio program "Prophetic Views Behind The News", hosted by Jan Markell, KKMS 980-AM

Rudy Giuliani

"THEY talk about sleep deprivation. I mean, on that theory, I'm getting tortured running for President of the United States. That's plain silly."

» What is he: 2008 Republican presidential candidate
» Where is he from: New York
» Date of quote: November 3, 2007

Source: Interview with Al Hunt--joking about torture

John Boehner

"DESPITE our offers to work together, Speaker Nancy Pelosi and Majority Leader Harry Reid are pushing ahead with backroom negotiations to draw up a trillion-dollar government takeover of health care from several Democratic bills. These plans include a number of troubling proposals that all seniors need to be aware of, including a $500 billion cut to Medicare, and a $172 billion cut to Medicare Advantage."

»   What is he: GOP House Republican Leader
»   Where is he from: Ohio
»   Date of quote: October 22, 2009

Source: John Boehner's website.. http://www.politico.com/livepulse/

Don Rumsfeld

Picture on the right is Sgt. Ivan Frederick sitting on an Iraqi detainee between two stretchers

(picture on the right is Sgt. **Ivan Frederick** sitting on an Iraqi detainee between two stretchers)

"I stand for 8-10 hours a day. Why is standing limited to four hours?"

»   What is he: Former U.S. Secretary of Defense
»   Where is he from: Texas
»   Date of quote: June 24, 2004

Source' http://www.usatoday.com/news/washington/2004-06-22-rumsfeld-abuse-usat_x.htm

2nd Source: Written on a memo in reference to the treatment of Guantanamo prisoner and to the way he worked in his office as Secretary of Defense, 2002. Reported in The Washington Post, 24 June 2004.[11]

Brit Hume

"IT'S time a few things be said about him," (Rep. John Murtha's (D-PA) "This guy is long past the day when he had anything but the foggiest awareness of what the heck is going on in the world." "absolute fountain" of "naïveté."

» What is he: Fox News senior political analyst
» Where is he from: Fox Cable News
» Date of quote: February 18, 2007

Source: Broadcasting Co.'s Fox News

Lindsey Graham

"I was incredibly disappointed in the tone of his speech." "At times, I found his tone to be overly combative and believe he behaved in a manner beneath the dignity of the office. I fear his speech tonight has made it more difficult – not less – to find common ground.

» What is he: U.S. Senator
» Where is he from: South Carolina
» Date of quote: September 9, 2009

Source: http://www.politico.com/news/stories/0909/26970.html. President Barack Obama. "address to Congress"

Samuel Wurzelbacher AKA, Joe the Plumber

"A vote for Obama is a vote for the death of Israel."

»   What is he: An unlicensed plumber
»   Where is he from: Ohio
»   Date of quote: October 29,2008

Source: WorldNetDaily: 2008 Presidential rally in Ohio

Dick Cheney

(Holder to launch a probe into alleged abuse of prisoners under the prior administration) "OFFENDS the hell out of me"

» What is he: Previous Vice President
» Where is he from: Wyoming
» Date of quote: August 30, 2009

Source: http://www.foxnews.com/politics/2009/08/30/cheney-slams-obamas-politicized-probe-cia-interrogations/

Liz Cheney

"PERHAPS Mr. Obama thinks he is making America inoffensive to our enemies. In reality, he is emboldening them and weakening us. America can be disarmed literally – by cutting our weapons systems and our defensive capabilities – as Mr. Obama has agreed to do. We can also be disarmed morally by a president who spreads false narratives about our history or who accepts, even if by his silence, our enemies' lies about us."

» What is she: Former Deputy Assistant Secretary of State
» Where is she from: Virginia
» Date of quote: July 13, 2009

Source: Wall Street Journal http://online.wsj.com/article/
SB124744075427029805.html

Karl Rove

"CONSERVATIVES saw the savagery of 9/11 in the attacks and prepared for war; liberals saw the savagery of the 9/11 attacks and wanted to prepare indictments and offer therapy and understanding for our attackers."

» What is he: President George W. Bush's chief strategist
» Where is he from: Colorado
» Date of quote: June 23, 2005

Source: New York Times.. http://www.nytimes.com/2005/06/23/politics/23rove.html

Anthony Robert Martin-Trigona AKA Andy Martin

"I am able to understand how the Holocaust took place, and with every passing day feel less and less sorry that it did."

» What is he: 2010 Republican candidate for U.S. Senator
» Where is he from: Connecticut
» Date of quote: August 3, 2009

Source: http://en.wikipedia.org/wiki/Andy_Martin_(U.S._politician)

Mitt Romney

"FOCUSING solely on jobs created while ignoring the far greater numbers of jobs lost is Harry Houdini economics."

- » What is he: Former Governor
- » Where is he from: Massachusetts
- » Date of quote: December 4, 2009

Source: http://www.boston.com/news/nation/articles/2009/12/04/

Jon Kyle

(Recovery Act) "THE Senate would do us all a great favor if it started again from scratch."

- » What is he: U.S. Senator
- » Where is he from: Arizona
- » Date of quote: February 4, 2009

Source: http://videocafe.crooksandliars.com/heather/thom-hartmann-im-dizzy-do-republican-alway

Newt Gingrich

FACT....WASHINGTON – Former House Speaker Newt Gingrich was having an extramarital affair even as he led the charge against President Clinton over the Monica Lewinsky affair.

» What is he: Former Speaker of the U.S. House of Representatives
» Where is he from: Pennsylvania
» Date acknowledging having affair during Clinton impeachment: March 8, 2007

Source: http://www.foxnews.com/story/0,2933,258001,00.html

Dick Cheney

"MY belief is we will, in fact, be greeted as liberators."

» What is he: Previous Vice President
» Where is he from: Wyoming
» Date of quote: November 14, 2003

Source: Meet the Press... http://www.msnbc.msn.com/id/3080244/

Tom DeLay

"THE most irresponsible, hypocritical speech I have ever witnessed," and that what Obama is talking about doing is "insane."

- » What is he: Former House Republican Whip
- » Where is he from: Texas
- » Date of quote: February 25, 2009

Source: http://www.huffingtonpost.com/2009/02/25/tom-delay-slams-obamas-ad_n_170016.html

John McCain

"I'M trying to do the Lord's work in the city of Satan against Obamacare," he said. "What this amounts to is generational theft."

» What is he: U.S. Senator
» Where is he from: Arizona
» Date of quote: March 31, 2010

Source: http://www.yourwestvalley.com/articles/mccain-14587-reform-health.html

Mitt Romney

"I'M glad they don't have access to lawyers", huh? "I think we should double Guantanamo."

» What is he: Former Governor
» Where is he from: Massachusetts
» Date of quote: May 17, 2007

Source: YouTube..www.youtube.com/watch?v=I0U9k7Jj_40

Liz Cheney

"IT is irresponsible for an American president to go to Moscow and tell a room full of young Russians less than the truth about how the Cold War ended. One wonders whether this was just an attempt to push "reset" – or maybe to curry favor. Perhaps, most concerning of all, Mr. Obama believes what he said."

» What is she: Former Deputy Assistant Secretary of State
» Where is she from: Virginia
» Date of quote: July 13, 2009

Source: Wall Street Journalhttp://exposingliberallies.blogspot.com/2009/07/liz-cheney-exposes-obamas-lies.html

Newt Gingrich

"POLITICS and war are remarkably similar situations. I think one of the great problems we have in the Republican Party is that we don't encourage you to be nasty. We encourage you to be neat, obedient, loyal and faithful and all those Boy Scout words, which would be great around a campfire but are lousy in politics."
"Democrats are the enemy of normal Americans."

» What is he: Former Speaker of the U.S. House of Representatives
» Where is he from: Pennsylvania
» Date of quote: February 6, 2009

Source: BrainyQuote// http://www.nutquote.com/quote/Newt_Gingrich/

President Barack Obama

Thank you, President Obama, for continuing to fight the negative ideology of "The Party of Hell No." Your hard work to improve the lives of all Americans is truly appreciated.

Acknowledgments

We would like to thank Jeff for pointing out a quote or two that made him scream, "I can't believe they said that," constantly inspiring us to go on, but mostly for his ability to catch spelling errors. We would like to thank Cody, Matt and Nick for practicing tolerance, fairness, compassion and equality in their day to day lives, frequently with the use of strong sarcasm and dark humor.

And thank you to Judy for her passionate debates, her astute political hilarity and uncanny optimism for America's future.

Last, we would like to give recognition to the GOP aka PHN, for speaking out loud, explaining in their own words, what true Republican principles, agendas, morality and ethics are all about.

About the Authors

Dianne and Glenn are the creators of the website ThePartyofHellNo. Net.

Dianne is an accountant. She was born into the Air Force, lived in Germany, traveled throughout Europe and America. She now lives with her husband, Jeff, in California. They both share a strong interest in politics.

Glenn, the father of two teenage boys, works in a Medical laboratory, making sure your test results are correct. He was raised in California, but has lived and traveled to many states. He also shares a passion for politics.

Disclaimer

We apologize to anyone who has been misquoted. Our goal was never to distort or misrepresent any one. Our intent was to show true Republican view points in their own words. Our sources come from highly regarded world and local newspapers, web and video sharing sites, and many cable news and local television stations. We have also attended various live speeches and political events.

Index

www.ingramcontent.com/pod-product-compliance
Lightning Source LLC
Chambersburg PA
CBHW062136280526
45788CB00001B/182